LIBERAL RACISM
CREATES THE BLACK
CONSERVATIVE

LIBERAL RACISM CREATES THE BLACK CONSERVATIVE

✦

Issues and New Perspectives

LUCKY ROSENBLOOM

Member-State Council On Black Minnesotans. Chair-Black
Republican Coalitian of Minnesota. President-Black
Conservative Committee of Minnesota.

iUniverse, Inc.
New York Lincoln Shanghai

Liberal Racism Creates the Black Conservative
Issues and New Perspectives

iUniverse books may be ordered through booksellers or by contacting:

iUniverse
2021 Pine Lake Road, Suite 100
Lincoln, NE 68512
www.iuniverse.com
1-800-Authors (1-800-288-4677)

ISBN-13: 978-0-595-40033-1 (pbk)
ISBN-13: 978-0-595-84415-9 (ebk)
ISBN-10: 0-595-40033-7 (pbk)
ISBN-10: 0-595-84415-4 (ebk)

Printed in the United States of America

To my family

May love, joy and peace of God, surround my family. Fruits of the spirit to my deceased parents, that gave me the spirit of self-reliance. For giving me the character of a winner opposed to being a victim. My father that taught me that being a real Black man means keeping your word. Because if your word is nothing you are nothing. My mother that always advised me to be honest and stay out of trouble. My father, that taught me to be strong. My mother, that taught me to be forgiving. I have all of your spirits. I shall meet you in heaven.

My mom taught me not to die without being everything God would want me to be, without having everything God would want me to have. I shall join you in heaven.

Police Memoriam
God be with the families of Officers killed in the line of duty.
The spirit of holiness rest with the spirit of each Officer

CONTENTS

PREFACE

The truth about Bill Clinton

Warning: Reading this column could cause stress and anxiety for liberals

Why is it that not one Black leader attacked Clinton on his actions on social issues in 1993, when many of his positions followed the conservative and Republican ideology? Clinton sponsored one of the most punitive crime bills in history. Clinton signed one of the most punitive welfare reform bills in history.

Republicans only talked about doing such things, and Blacks called Republicans racist because these acts would affect poor mothers and have an adverse impact on Black thugs. Clinton would advocate and sign these bills into law, yet he would visit Black churches and people loved the man. Heck! Clinton could have revived slavery and some Blacks would have yelled, "Amen, brother!"

One of Clinton's most favored ideas was his economic stimulus package. I remember hearing some of our leaders begging for this one, because it contained funds for urban development. This would have created jobs for the urban gatekeepers after creating havoc and living off the urban poor as they create jobs for themselves.

Blacks hated Republicans for wanting to change Affirmative Action, which, in my opinion, has destroyed Blacks with its group victimization and inferior stigma. Nevertheless, Clinton would visit Black churches with his "mend it, don't fix it" hip-hop rap. The Black liberals became his hype crew, or didn't say a word. Well, it's been fixed all right.

Clinton tricked Blacks by visiting Africa, playing the sexophone (I mean saxophone), and praying with Blacks in our churches. This conservative and other Black conservatives were not thunderstruck or tricked. Right here in Minnesota, I and other Black conservatives warned the liberal Black leaders (most refused to accept that they have led our community into dependency doom) that Clinton's policies would have an unconstructive impact on the poorest Blacks.

Clinton's crime bill and his welfare reform bill have led to increased criminalization of Black youth. Under Clinton's policies, Blacks have witnessed poor Blacks entering the labor market without skills and no real investment in our communities or schools. Liberal Blacks with White support would blame Republicans when Clinton visited the Black churches, NAACP and the Urban League.

In the Black church, Clinton must have asked, "Lord Jesus, why do these Blacks love me so much? Surely, they must see what I have done? Please Lord, if it is your will, keep them blind until after my administration."

I am sure Clinton in many of his speeches at Black churches and organizations wanted to ask, "What is it brothers? Why do you all love me so much? I don't have any Blacks in my cabinet, or few in key positions. I have done little for you. Wuz up with this love?"

Clinton played on his perception of Blacks. Let me explain: Clinton knew well that no other people within the national electorate have given more time, hard work and dedication to the Democratic Party than Blacks. Clinton knew Blacks had no options other than Republicans. Blacks bashing Republicans with liberal support would be hypocritical to turn and ask Republicans for help against Clinton's policies.

This is the box Black liberal leadership has put us into, and this has been poor leadership. Clinton got away with hurting Blacks more than any other president in the past 40 years, including Ronald Reagan (his policies actually helped Blacks), because we had no options. Expressing loyalty to Democrats only has led us to being sophisticated beggars.

As I've sated in my previous columns, I am going to continue to write about liberal racism because there is a lot to write about nationally and locally. I express my appreciation to many of you who have seen the truth in my observations.

Ask yourself this question: For over 40 years we you have had problems in your community while under the control of Democrats at all levels of government. Why?

My intent with the compilation of opinions as a conservative radio talk show host and columnist is to provide intellectual, yet harrowing opinions surrounding social conditions which allow individuals the ability perpetuate liberal political racism in communities of color.

Most people have discourse behind closed doors in agreement with my opinions. Some are afraid to talk about my observations in public because they fear creating enemies within the Democrat Party. White liberals are afraid to debate because of the truth within my profound opinions. Black liberals are afraid to debate my opinions because I do not fit into the stereotype of what they have promulgated the Black conservative as being.

The outdated liberal leadership confronted by young conservatives and our challenging opinions rush to silence our growing population of self-reliance removing dependency on liberal policies that have destroyed Black families. The archaic assemblage of liberal gatekeepers is bemused as the growing number of Blacks, are looking at other political affiliations in a move away from liberal dependency to self-reliance and economic security.

Democrats seem mystified, wondering the best possible means to regain control of this evolution of Black political change as Blacks across the country join other political affiliations. This dilemma causes social and political ramifications as Democrats attempt to regain control over their modern day liberal dependent constituents. When their attempts fail, Democrats will shame attempt to shame Blacks stepping outside the liberal restrictions by using the tools of guilt, shame, and calling conservatives Uncle Toms.

Democrats rush to deal with Black women that identify with Condaleezza Rice and other strong conservatives of color. This, with the idea that most Blacks, once educated, become conservative think tanks across the country, leaves the liberal Democrat trying to develop strategies to regain control over the new, well educated Black conservative. Liberals find the Black conservative unpredictable and incapable of control because we fail to recognize the White liberal as the savior of Black people. In fact, we view many of their policies as destructive to our families and community. The old-school liberal racism is not prepared to deal with the newly developed political schemes of the new Black conservative.

I provide my opinions because there is a need to expose liberal racism in communities of color and to start people looking at politics at the local, state and federal levels. After doing so, realizing that liberals have controlled their communities for years, but the social depravations, poor education, crime, joblessness and more, continues. Republicans do not control your communities, liberal have the control. Take the blame where the blame is, not outside your communities to Republicans. The blame falls on the liberal Democrats that have controlled your community for decades.

What makes this book controversial is a hard look at the truth. Exposing liberal policies that have destroyed Black families such as welfare. Welfare has destroyed the Black family. The criteria by which one must qualify to receive benefits such as the absence of the father, has a scary similarity to the removal of the Black man from his spouse during slavery.

It is my desire that liberals will gain knowledge from my opinions and move toward undoing racist dependency and dehumanizing policies that harm Black people. My opinions must motivate Black conservatives to speak out and move our country toward self-reliance and less dependency on government. We must not continue to depend on government to solve our problems because we shall be dependent on that scarcity of resources, thus begging for four hundred more years. The Black conservative is the innovative voice for our future and we must not be silenced by the use of shame, being called White, or Uncle Toms because we have the courage to step off the liberal plantation of control and dependency.

My parents were strong Black people that grew up under the Jim Crow laws of the South. My parents migrated to Minnesota with only five-dollars among themselves, traveling on a freight train. This Black couple would become legends in Minnesota raising eight children from a business housed in a small tin shack for over fifty-seven years. My parents never accepted welfare, loans or government handouts. At their deaths, their business was moved to the Minnesota Historical Society for viewing and the street where their business was located is named after them an act of our city council. To learn more about our historic family go to google.com Using quotations to limit your search conduct three searches. Type in "Lucky Rosenbloom," my father's name "Tiger Jack Rosenbloom" and my mother's name "Nurceal Rosenbloom"

ACKNOWLEDGEMENTS

I would be careless not to offer my sincere appreciation to the Minnesota Spokesman-Recorder Newspaper for allowing my opinions to be expressed in our "Issues and New Perspectives Column." I urge the reader to call and subscribe to this paper to read my future columns/opinions at 612 827.4021

SAGACITY 1
WE MUST DROP THE VICTIM ROLE TO PROSPER

We must ask ourselves the question, "Why is it that other people from different cultures have achieved substantial economic gains, higher education levels, higher home and business ownership as compared to African Americans?"

There are three reasons: (1) The federal, state, and local liberal politicians who control our community; (2) Black community leaders who make excuse after excuse for their blunders, and who by doing so have excused our people into becoming victims of blame and doom; and (3) we have failed to give up the acceptance of victimization that is so intensely highly wrought in our culture.

Now, the victim position has failed because we have no real negotiation based within the liberal structure. We are duped into believing that White blame will manifest into business opportunities. The liberals have not and will not let go of White dispensation in our communities. Black leadership must realize that the concept of guilt premeditated at White liberals has a deceptive perception of power. White liberals have used this guilt game as a way to oppress us economically.

Other cultures not experienced in the guilt game gather themselves collectively to create business and economic opportunity. This independence allows these cultures to thrive. Our leaders have led us into doom while excusing this direction as our being victims deserving of welfare and other destructive liberal benefits. By being victims, Blacks have lost their sense of self-reliance. We depend on White liberals to rescue us. White liberals need this victim mentality to offer dependency programs, which gives them a sense of repentance from the wrongs projected on Blacks since slavery. This victim mentality matched with the repentance response can be seen in Affirmative Action, preferences, and other liberal policies after the civil rights movement. We have been taught dependency, opposed to self-reliance, which is the reason Blacks fail to create businesses as do other newly arriving cultures in our own communities.

1

The new liberal electronic form of discrimination

Young Blacks, and one Black woman in particular, have reported to me that most corporations are now accepting job applications via e-mail/internet. The information goes through a database. The database selects key words for the selected position.

Anyone who makes it through this process is sent an electronic application and could be discriminated against based on one's cultural name, ethnicity, or community. Thus, living in predominantly Black areas under the control of liberals equals discrimination. Liberals are aware of this practice within their communities, but have done nothing to seriously challenge this practice. If get by this discriminatory practice to an interview, the job description suddenly changes outside of the required qualifications of your background that initially got you the interview.

This woman believes that she receives calls from potential employers after going through the electronic process, and if a voice message is left on an answering machine with her standard voice mail greeting, the potential employer leaves a message for a date and time for the interview. Once the woman returns the call, this is when liberal discrimination begins. Oh! The name Jill Scottishberg is White, however, she sounds like a Black person. The woman reported that this practice is taking place not outside, but inside her community within a liberal operated entity.

I want to thank the woman that shared her experience for this section. This is the most hidden and protected discrimination occurring in communities of color that are under liberal and Democratic control.

President Clinton educated the liberal racist

The cool brother Clinton, the "first Black president," in his 1997 inaugural speech asked over one million college folks to read to America's children. Slick Clinton was using a well-known Democrat paradigm of White hope liberalism to create White power by establishing the Black reading problem as a stipulation that implied that the White liberal teacher is hope for the poor student. This was a slick way of fostering the myth of affirmative action, which is often seen as a way to help the marginal Black.

A question given to the Mayor of Minneapolis

Since the Iraq War began, we have had 30 Minnesotans killed serving our country. Since 2001, we have had 224 homicides in Minneapolis. Two White men were killed in business areas at the hands of criminals of color.

Where are the Black leaders to challenge Rybak, to have discourse about his loud action for more police and resources when people of color are killing people of color? The liberal Mayor has demonstrated White hope liberal racism, yet no Black leader made a serious issue of this inept action. Why? Because they are wearing min-skirts and hot pants and are afraid to speak out for fear of losing any crumbs given in the past to keep the Black warriors from becoming conservative.

In 2004, the violent crime rate for Minneapolis was more than two and a half times the national average. The murder rate for the nation was 5.5 per 100, 0000. This author does not claim to be an expert, or even good in math, but this means that the Minneapolis rate was almost three times the national average, 14.1 per 100,000.

The FBI statistics indicate an increase in crime in Murderapo—I mean, Minneapolis. Crime across the nation decreased while crime here increased. Mayor Rybak, where were you before the 2006 Uptown and Block E killings? All of these crimes occur under the liberal DFL-controlled community. What is being done? Read the Mayor's response a bit later.

SAGACITY 2
MINNEAPOLIS PUBLIC SCHOOL'S
SUPERINTENDENT—FORCED
OFF THE PLANTATION?

The Minneapolis Pubic Schools Superintendent lynched by liberals as community member's yelled racism. One of our Black leaders Randy Staten, had to force his way to the podium, saying, "Take me to jail," because the liberals at the podium attempted to prevent the voices of Black folks and Black leaders from being heard at a meeting to fire the Minneapolis superintendent. Then, with an old plantation move pitting Blacks against Blacks, the liberals would bring out their ammunition by introducing another Black person to replace a Black woman, being fired. Sounds like something happening in your area? If Republicans acted as such, folks would scream racism. However, under the double standard of ignorance, liberal discriminate and folks are silent..

Look at the history of racism in your community. Remember your own experience with racism. Remember all the times you've heard about and/or experienced racism in your community—has it not been by the hands of liberals and Democrats? Our so-called male leaders have dressed in hot pants and mini-skirts, and the cuties have switched through it all over the years doing, or saying little. I'll explain the reasons for this inability to respond as you read further..

SAGACITY 3
A LETTER TO OUR MAYOR OF
MUDERAPOLIS

The Honorable Mayor
R.T. Rybak of Minneapolis

Since the war in Iraq we have had up to **30** military personnel killed serving our country. The number of homicides in your city (Minneapolis) since September 2001 has been **224**.

Considering the above, many feel your **urgency** to address homicides is because of **two-Whites** being **killed by people of color** in the Uptown and Block E areas, and because Gov. Pawlenty's confronting this matter.

The Mayor's unedited Response:

Assaults that have led to murder are deplorable, regardless of where they occurred. While no part of the city is immune to this problem, certain areas are suffering more. Regardless of where the media decides to focus, I have made clear that reducing crime in north Minneapolis is my top priority and essential to the city's success. I understand the impact crime has because I spend a lot of time in neighborhoods meeting with residents and discussing solutions.

Public safety has been my top priority for resources and that will not change. We are adding 71 police officers this year, putting more officers on the street than any point since 2001. We are also increasing police visibility and presence, meaning residents will see more cops and talk to more cops in their neighborhood. Cops will be getting out of their cars, out of their routines and inserting themselves into the community, building relationships with residents.

We are establishing a Safety Center on West Broadway. Our South Side and North Side Robbery Task Forces are contributing police presence in areas with the greatest robbery patterns. We are creating a new Juvenile Unit in the police department to coordinate youth enforcement and work with schools to centralize juvenile crime prevention.

We also need to get upstream on the root causes of crime. We can't arrest the problem of crime away. There is a time for tough enforcement—and we will do that—but we also must prevent crime by creating an environment of hope to attack the core issues of jobs, housing, and youth engagement.

Mayor R.T. Rybak

Lucky Responds:

I want to address the last paragraph of the Mayor's response in particular the identification of joblessness as a reason for crime.

We will always have joblessness—not because jobs are not available, but because of the liberal public policies that reproduces a culture of people that are conditioned not to work and settle for just getting by. Public policies that create fathers that are irresponsible and mothers that accept the victim mentality whereby, liberal systems are seen as their savior, hope and only means of survival. Welfare, like slavery has destroyed the Black family and the individual Black spirit of self-reliance. Welfare has been equal to slavery because of it's long-term dependency outcomes. Like slavery-recipients need to have babies for eligibility, fathers could not live with the family, or risk being sanctioned, workers could come in and separate siblings, and you could not have a job. Thus welfare creates joblessness and kills the Black spirit, motivation, self-reliance and motivation to look for jobs.

Welfare creates crime because within the family it sustains the inability to learn work skills. Living on results in poor education because educators lack the ability to teach students with low self-esteem. Family members within the welfare family system often do not desire, or have the motivation to shift from joblessness toward work. The manifestations of welfare perpetuate crime. The liberal response to address joblessness and not the causes of joblessness being dependency policies-offers the liberal freedom from accepting that welfare policies are the root of both crime and joblessness. Welfare is implemented to clear White liberal guilt and to keep constituents. End welfare and put people to work by creating affirmative access to jobs training, education and job opportunities. Welfare is the underpinning process toward joblessness. Conservatives have the right agenda with our welfare time limits, our mandate to work within a given time period, or lose benefits drive has help move mothers to meaningful job and other worthy opportunities. Working as a counselor in one such program, I witnessed recipients becoming nurses, teachers, and more. Teaching in public schools, I have seen siblings change from hopelessness to migrating toward improvement because of seeing their parents working. Get the idea Mayors across the country?

Without hyperbolizing, I offer that the majority of youth crime is committed by youth living in welfare recipient families. Start with this variable of welfare, or we will continue to pump money into programs and policies that only foster crime, helplessness and shame within families across America.

SAGACITY 4
MALCOLM X WOULD VOTE FOR BUSH

Malcolm X said in his 1960s speech "*The Ballot or the Bullet*" that if one political party is Black people's enemy; the other doesn't have to be their friend. He even called Democrats "*racist Dixiecrats.*"

The Democrats' welfare system is equal to slavery. Let's look at welfare guidelines. One must have babies. The woman can't have a man living with her. The woman can't have a meaningful job. And at one time a social worker could come in and separate the Black family shifting siblings to some far off unknown location. Sounds like slavery to me.

Malcolm X once told a group of sisters, "*Allah does not want you on welfare, and Allah wants you to work.*" The enemy, as Malcolm implied, is the creation of dependency programs by the Democrats that have reproduced poverty and the destruction of the Black family.

Why would Malcolm X vote for Bush? The answer is simple. President Bush offers a decidedly more optimistic vision of what Black America can accomplish. Should Kerry be elected, we will no longer see Blacks such as Ms. Rice representing America within the media, as we do today. We will see fewer people of color in the powerful cabinet positions as today.

The Kerry ticket will take Black people back to the 1800s and the same type of government dependency programs that have destroyed the gains of our Black families, businesses and communities. Malcolm X would not vote for this type of future for Black people.

President Bush would raise the standard of living for Black America by bringing authentic ideas toward economic growth. The president's economic policies have allowed Black Americans to weather the stock market bubble, the recession, the terrorist attack, and the corporate scandals and have resulted in higher incomes and living standards for Black people.

President Bush has created 13 million new jobs since the start of July 2004. In Minnesota, we have seen nearly 25,000 new jobs, dropping the unemployment rate to 4.4 percent from five percent a year ago. Black people are working and creating more businesses in our community because of self-reliance.

We have seen personal income of Blacks swell. In Minnesota, we have witnessed an increase of 1.4 percent to $178.2 billion during the first quarter of 2004. We can't blame our failure to keep this money in our community on the White man. Malcolm X would expect Blacks to unite around the monetary growth.

Under President Bush's policies, we see home ownership higher than any other time throughout the history of Black home ownership. In the first quarter of this year, home ownership remained at the record high of 68.8 percent. Here in the Twin Cities, Black home ownership is on the rise.

Another four years of President Bush would allow for more productivity in the Black community. Productivity grew at the fastest rate in more than 50 years.

We are winning the war on terror by bringing the war to the terrorists. We are protecting Black families with the passage of the USA PATRIOT Act. We shall continue the quest toward independence vs. dependency on government that has crippled Black people.

This is likely to be the closest election in Minnesota history, and the Black vote, the vote of all people of color, shall be the controlling factor. Let's stop begging the Democrats and work toward less dependency on the Democrat welfare programs that have destroyed our women, families and communities.

An African Proverb: "*A people that cannot help themselves are lost forever.*" This only has meaning when people move away from liberal dependency policies toward self-reliance.

SAGACITY 5
GAY MARRIAGE ISSUE NOT COMPARABLE TO CIVIL RIGHTS MOVEMENT

The comparison of gay marriages to the struggle for civil/voting rights is wrong. This comparison is nefarious and will allow distortion in the history of the struggle of Black people if left unchallenged in today's society.

Let me explain myself. The gay rights issue is easily associated with the civil rights due to the appearance of people being subjugated. However, any White gay person continues to enjoy the White privilege guaranteed in a race-based society created to benefit White people during the reconstruction.

Fact: If a gay White simply refuses to act gay, he/she shall enjoy the benefits of a race-based society. Now, this same opportunity will not be given to a gay Black, regardless if that person acts gay or not. Thus the gay issue cannot be associated with civil rights. Most Black liberals will accept this position. However, because most Blacks are locked into the liberal bars of prison, they will allow the gay/civil rights association in full disrespect to our brothers and sisters who were killed in our struggle.

All one must do is explore this matter with heavier scrutiny toward understanding the civil rights and voting rights movements relevant to ascribe status, and not one's choice of sin. The concept of gay marriage may appear to be a civil rights issue only because this is the spin gay supporters manipulate and integrate into civil rights.

However, closer understanding will allow most Blacks to accept gay marriage not as an issue of civil/voting rights, but as an issue of "sanctioning our sins rights" because it is about a choice, it's about behavior in clear contradiction to most Black Christians who are truly into the word of God. Didn't God create Adam and Eve, not Adam and Steve?

All right, I may have failed in that bit of humor. But at issue is the question, "Is gay marriage about behavior, or ethnicity?" If your answer is behavior, gay marriage cannot be associated with civil rights/voting rights. The argument that the two share anything in common lacks substance.

Question: Why is there an attempt to associate gay marriages with the Civil Rights Movement? The answer is simple: The Civil Rights Movement was a powerful movement toward change. The Civil Rights Movement, with the support of our Lord Jesus Christ, brought down some of the most evil people throughout our history. Thus to have gays integrate this issue is a good fit.

A lot of good people, Black and White, women and men and children, died together for civil/voting rights. The equation becomes, a good movement equals sympathy. Black people ought not allow this sinful attachment to our continuous struggle.

Brown v. Board of Education

As a practicing paralegal, and social studies teacher, I feel it's important to educate our people about court cases that have impacted our lives. One such case is Brown v. Board of Education, 347 U.S. 483 (1954).

Significance: This ruling reversed the Supreme Court's earlier position on segregation set by Plessey v. Ferguson (1896). The decision also inspired congress and the federal courts to help carry our further civil rights reforms for African Americans.

Background: Beginning in the 1930s, the National Association for the Advancement of Colored People (NAACP) began using the courts to challenge racial segregation in public education. In 1952 the NAACP took a number of school segregation cases to the Supreme Court. These included the Brown's family suit against the school board of Topeka, Kansas, over its "separate-but-equal" policy.

Decisions: The case was decided on May 17, 1954, by a vote of 9 to 0. Chief Justice Earl Warren spoke for the unanimous court, which ruled that segregation in public education created inequality. The court held that racial segregation in public schools was by nature unequal, even if the school facilities were equal. The Court noted that such segregation created feelings of inferiority that could not be undone. Therefore, enforced separation of races in public education is unconstitutional.

Question: At a point in history, the Supreme Court issued a ruling that prohibited women from practicing law, saying that women were too timid and would best serve society by being home raising the children of their husbands. Which justice provided this written opinion?

SAGACITY 6
WILL THE DEMOCRATS BLOCK BLACK PROGRESS ONLY TO WIN FUTURE ELECTIONS?

The Bush Administration will provide insurmountable opportunities for people of color. It's sad that doomsday preachers are spreading messages that young people internalize and accept as another reason not to work hard toward success. Preaching doom, during Republican administrations.

Let me explain. I had a student that advised others in an assembly that life was over because of the reelection of President Bush. I looked at the student and asked several questions: Is Bush standing here, stopping you from obtaining your diploma? Did Bush tell any of you to come to school at 10 am when you were supposed to here at 8 am? Is Bush telling those of you in school right now, high on drugs, not to do your work, not to turn in your assignments, or to smoke that blunt during your class break?

Over 100 students appeared to reach catharsis as they listened with ownership for their own behavior instead of placing negative their own failing behaviors on President Bush. The doom-preaching liberals must discontinue spreading messages of helplessness because of their own adjustment to liberal government dependency.

Some of the people in our community that tell us how awful things under Bush drive expensive cars, wear expensive suits, eat at Red Lobster etc. I say loudly. Tell our poor people victims of Bush what you are doing to survive Republican administrations, and all will be fine.

Let's go over some issues in the coming months starting with Social Security. President Bush would maintain the solvency of the Social Security system by allowing younger workers to invest part of their payroll taxes in stocks or other savings. This is an opportunity for Black people to have both security and independence by owning more of their future.

The Democrats will argue that if younger people's taxes do not feed the system, this would force a tax increase or cuts in benefits. The Democrats argue that this would make the program private. Help me understand something liberals. What is wrong with Black folks owning something?

Let's look at education. President Bush argues that we must continue the work of education reform to bring high quality and accountability. We shall accomplish this by lifting the standards for teachers and raising student expectations, as seen in No Child Left Behind.

Oh no, says the liberal. The Democrats would delay this concept over meaningless details such as spending. What a cover up. The Democrats beat Republicans 99 to one raising taxes and spending your money. Now we have an education concept that will equal the learning playing field, and the Democrats worry about spending?

Doomsday preachers talk about the economy and job creation. In basic Economics 101, we learn that the best way to jumpstart the economy is to create more jobs while lowering the cost of health care for individuals and businesses. The way to do this is by streamlining laws and regulations affecting businesses. This is why Black conservatives and liberals have little to talk about. Liberals do not understand the Black conservative desire to get away from government control over our lives. Liberals believe that we need some source telling us what to do because we are incapable of self-reliance.

President Bush indicates the need to confront frivolous lawsuits that drive up cost of health care and have a negative impact on Black doctors and patients of color. However, in rides the Democrat and liberal doomsday preachers on their white horses, with expensive watches, and new homes, telling the Black community that Bush only wants to discourage lawsuits that are costly to businesses and doctors by limiting awards, thereby discouraging lawsuits. This is further manipulation by the liberals to block a presidential conservative concept benefiting Black people.

Oh! I almost forgot. A Black woman for the first time in history has been appointed to the highest presidential cabinet position ever. Let's thank President Clinton for this appointment? Did you get the sarcasm?

Thugs' thumbs be gone

I understand the frustration of homeowners throughout America falling victim to thugs damaging their garages, homes, automobiles and other property with spray paint depicting gang signs. When these thugs are apprehended and convicted, we need to cut off their thumbs.

Wouldn't this make it difficult for those convicted thugs to hold a paint can and cause further damage to property? We can call it the "Thumbs Off" legislation.

SAGACITY 7
LIBERAL RACISTS WILL NOT
GO TO HEAVEN

The liberal Christians beat Republican Christians 99-1 in the racism game. Slavery, starting in 1619, could never have existed without the support and/or tolerance of racism and prejudice by the Christian liberal onlookers.

History will show that the Ku Klux Klan platform called for the murder of Radical Republicans, not Christian Democrats. Liberal Christians supported slavery and the lynching of Blacks by the Ku Klux Klan through their evil interpretation of scripture.

Liberals created this White and Black thing centered on the real issue of sex, not wanting the Black man to mix with the White woman. This is the reason liberals in the South supported segregation and made Blacks out to be animals, inferior and not worthy of respect.

Someone has to talk about this issue, because in America racism is real and liberals have duped Blacks into believing that racism in America is a myth. Worse, the house Negro in our community helps to sustain this myth.

Most of you reading my opinions on this matter cannot believe that a Black conservative is discoursing on this matter with the courage to attack liberal racism. Black conservatives are best suited to bring this matter out in the open, because racist liberals have not subjugated us within the acceptance of what we social scientists view as the pseudo-scientific integrated philosophy of race that has been cleverly created and sustained based on the overall culture and easy deception of Americans established on a race-based society as far back as Reconstruction.

I continue to challenge any liberal to a debate regarding the theme of liberal racism that this author is promulgating throughout the history of America, the civil war and liberal Southern slavery. The fact is that liberal Democrats were slave owners and used the Bible as a tool of blessing for their ownership of humans, hangings and separation of families. Not one liberal has taken the challenge to debate. I leave it to you, the reader, as to why?

No doubt, many are talking behind closed doors, behind my back, afraid to directly challenge my ability to articulate liberal racism.

No Black liberal need apply for the challenge, because I shall not play the game of a Black feeling pressured to protect the liberal racist Democrat functioning well many of your own communities.

Liberal Christians said nothing in the late '60s and '70s when Blacks would get the living s**t kicked out of them for being areas limited to Whites only. Or, when Blacks could only go swimming at certain locations on Thursdays in our own neighborhoods, which Blacks would come to call *"Black Night"* after which the White liberals would clean the pools and keep us out until the next Thursday. Oh yeah, this and much more was going on at the hands of liberals in our own communities.

Let us take a look at our community under the control of liberal politicians at all levels of government. I listen to Black leaders complain about poor housing, high taxes that force Blacks out of their homes, lack of jobs in our communities, mothers on welfare and fathers being kicked out of their homes in fear of losing benefits. Blacks not learning in schools, and more. Liberal politicians attend our churches and meetings, and Blacks talk about these matters as if some outside force is responsible.

Stand up and take off your miniskirts and hot pants. The people who are responsible are in your presence—the liberals that control our schools and some of our churches.

I am going to advertise lectures throughout the country titled *"Racist people will not go to Heaven."* I'll talk about racism and its victims and tell stories about racism heard over the years.

Surprising to many is that the evildoers are mostly liberal and working in liberal entities in our communities. The Humphrey Job Corps Center where a teacher told a Native American student that he was a slow learner because he was on Native American time? Or, the center director who has a picture of a Confederate general on his wall. I have a lot of liberal racism to lecture on.

Since Blacks migrated North during the 1940s, they have battled and have accepted liberal racism like good slaves on the Liberal Plantation. We must accept the truth. The truth is that the suffering of Blacks has been developed and sustained by liberal Christian Democrats, not conservatives and/or Republicans. Radical Republicans were on the kill list of the Ku Klux Klan.

Now, we have the Black conservative. The Black conservatives are ready to stand strong and confront the subtle bigotry of racism that President Bush often talks about that holds down the Black young school learner, the Black achiever. The Black conservative is the spirit of the Radical Republicans.

How is it that racism can exist in our own community year after year? The answer is within our people, our leaders, the liberal concept of dependency. If you realistically think about it, you will have to accept the truth. The gatekeepers have been rewarded well. Now, the new Black man and woman are aware of many of the gatekeepers in our community and are calling their names loud and clear.

The liberal wall of urban racism is known. Thank God for our young generation standing strong, kicking down the walls of liberal racism. Be on the alert, liberal racists—most of the young people in our congregations see your thorns when you are speaking in our churches.

SAGACITY 8
WILLIE LYNCH PLAN FAILING THE DEMOCRATS

This sagacity is my attempt at assisting Black people in reaching their psychological/sociological cathartic growth whereby you, the reader, will experience an inner change. This change will allow you to vote in the coming elections for candidates that best represent your biblical teachings vs. being conditioned to vote Democrat only.

I am going to challenge you to begin a development of self-reliance that will guide you toward voting for any candidate, not because he/she is a Democrat or Republican, but centered on your understanding as a child of God matched with your biblical understanding.

If a candidate supports same-sex marriage, and this is contrary to your biblical teaching, yet you vote for that person because he/she is a Democrat, have you placed your loyalty to a party over God? Vote your values. In order to accomplish this, one must first free oneself from the bondage of the Democrat Plantation—from the lesson plans of Willie Lynch.

The Democrats would not want you to accept the reality that polls continue to indicate a trend toward conservative viewpoints among African Americans. Willie Lynch would allow you to believe that we must serve one powerful master—the Democrats whip.

Throughout our great nation, we are seeing African American conservatives' voting patterns changing. As the Democratic slave master witnesses our people joining and voting in various political associations, they begin to threaten us by taking away those dependency programs. The Black liberal whose job it is to keep us in line on the Democrat plantation steps forward and attacks the Black conservative in more hateful ways than the White liberal himself.

However, as we begin to witness Black conservatives sounding, looking and being strong Black conservative men/women, the Democrats know that this shall translate into votes for conservatives, benefiting the Republican Party.

Now, for my friends on the other side finding the above paragraph incredulous, all you have to do is free yourself from the "Willie Lynch Democrat machine" and go to the internet. Once you're keyed up, go to your favorite search engine and key in "Black Republicans" or "Black Conservatives." Don't let the Democrat ruler catch you reading this information, for he shall report you to the master liberal, and this could mean losing some programs, funding, and other liberal you-better-be-loyal, dependency-on-us programs.

The Willie Lynch plan is failing the Democrats, because younger Black people are embarrassed seeing older Black leaders always begging. Liberal Black leaders beg for more money when Democrats are in control, only later to beg please don't take our money when Republicans are in control.

Young people are tired of this begging to the liberal Democrat. Do for yourself. We have the capacity to pick up ourselves. However, the Democrats want you to depend on government (today's plantation).

Allow me to elucidate for those of you confused and/or ready to run to the liberal and snitch me out for what is being presented. Black liberals, with the assistance of the media, have used Clarence Thomas as the prototype of Black conservatism. Hell, I would not be a Black conservative if this dude were the only one provided to our people as a carbon copy for Black conservatism.

As we look at Colin Powell, Condoleeza Rice, Shelby Steele, Thomas Sowell, and other outspoken Black conservatives, including myself, we talk Black, walk Black, and stand undaunted, relevant to the struggle of our people. This begins to dismantle the Democrat plantation. Why? The answer is simple: The Willie Lynch lesson plan used by Democrats to once again vilify, dehumanize, and destroy Blacks, this time Black conservatives is no longer successful..

As I speak to young college students, most are stunned to hear me talk with such strong recognition about racism, slavery, the evil inflicted on our people, and the need to have strong non-begging, non-dependency on government to resolve our issues. They realize that being a Black conservative is not being Uncle Tom. Most are seeing clearly liberal racism within our communities at the hands of liberals, while being blamed on conservatives/Republicans that have no political control over the politics of our communities.

Being a Black conservative is about being a strong Black man/woman knowing yourself as a Black person, refusing to beg, but standing on our feet, not living on our knees, recognizing racism, but refusing to be victims and seeing White liberalism as our only hope. We are constructed on self-reliance with an inner spirit that reminds us to be all and have all that God would desire, and no person is strong enough to prevent us from those achievements. This scares the Willie

Lynches within the Democratic Party. Should Powell and/or Rice run for president or vice president, polls have shown that the number of Blacks voting the Republican ticket would increase markedly.

SAGACITY 9
LIBERAL RACISM BEATS CONSERVATIVES' 99 TO ONE

Send back the Hispanics performing jobs that others will not? What about the White blonde-haired blue-eyed immigrant from Poland and other areas that blend into America working construction jobs? You all are thinking that Lucky is one bold Black conservative.

We fight for equality in Iraq while we have racism in America

President Bush said, *"America at our best values the life we see in one another, and must always remember that even the unwanted have worth. And our country must abandon all of the habits of racism because we cannot carry the message of freedom and the baggage of bigotry at the same time."*

Since I was a kid, it seemed that everyone that perpetrated some act of racism directed at myself and/or others has been a Democrat. I am aware of liberals who will be on trial soon for such actions as telling a Native American with learning difficulties that he was not getting anything done because he was on Native American time in a liberal school setting.

Or, there's the director of the same location having a picture in his office depicting Robert E. Lee, and the same director yelling at a Black woman in a meeting with others present. Many will witness liberal racism at the coming trial filed by one of a few Lawyers not afraid to challenge liberal racism.

Some of the most morally repugnant acts of racism upon people of color have been at the hands of Democrats, including the Duluth lynching in Minnesota. You won't believe some of the complaints we receive in our Civil Rights Law and History Center of racism in liberal entities. I challenge any reader to disprove that anywhere, 99 percent of people who discriminate in violation of the Title VII

Civil Rights Act of 1964 are Democrats and liberals in entities located in urban areas.

It's sickening that some Black leaders have been so subjugated, have become so dependent on the Democrat machine, that they are like men in hot pants and miniskirts, afraid to fight for people who have no voice or money or lack general knowledge of our justice system.

If only we had more strong brothers willing to fight and not close their eyes on liberal racism handed out by the hands of the Democrat machine gunners. We are blessed to have non-liberal and/or conservatives in positions of power in local Human Rights Departments. These non-liberals are not under control of liberals and their jobs have not become their God because of the independence firmly planted within their souls.

The Democrats, the liberals have always controlled our communities. Some-one please help me understand why we are complaining about the same things today, that we have complained about 20 years ago? One does not have to go far. Search your areas. Look at the social depravations, the plethora of hurting issues, all while under the control of liberal Democrats. Liberals must accept and imple-ment President Bush's remarks.

Democrats in your community must take off their hot pants and miniskirts and be dynamic in attacking liberal racism that is laid on the doorsteps of Repub-licans. I shall debate Democrat, liberal racism with anyone, at any time. Look at the problems occurring in your communities that never seem to end. The liberals control our communities at every level of government. Democrats beat Republi-cans at the racism game 99 to one.

Unlike some, I'll criticize my own party

I wonder why President Bush would go to visit a place as dangerous as Iraq, but found security issues when it came to visiting Americans at the New Orleans sta-dium during Hurricane Katrina? We Republicans have the unique ability to crit-icize each other, yet work together toward our final objectives, thus learning from criticism within.

But don't you Democrats dare do the same, for you may lose some money for your dependency programs that have destroyed Black women such as welfare. Worse, you may find yourselves extricated from the liberal affiliation of Demo-crats. Catharsis. I have discovered the reason some of you are afraid to speak out against community liberal racism. The fear of losing government dependency and other entitlement programs.

Liberal racism in the news

You've seen the news both in the papers and on television. Why are Black cocaine users who commit murder and other crimes shown as evil, nefarious and deserving of their criminal sentences, while White meth users who commit cold-blooded murders and other criminal acts are shown as coming from loving families falling victim to drugs? Drugs are accepted as some kind of social ailing for White drug users, while offered as no excuse for Black criminal behaviors. Read your local liberal newspaper. Watch your local liberal news. You'll figure this one out on your own.

SAGACITY 10
PRESIDENT OFFERS RELIEF
FOR HURRICANE VICTIMS

✦

LIBERALS OPPOSE MEASURES JUST
BECAUSE BUSH PROPOSES THEM

I volunteered a lot of time to the Hurricane relief center located on Energy Park Drive in St. Paul, Minnesota. The many people I talked with young, middle aged, the old, maintained and expressed faith in God. It was a learning experience talking to so many elders. Most seem to want to talk more about their families, the good times of growing up; the retired talked about their jobs and so many other memories that elders talk about.

Most of the evacuees of New Orleans had the spirit of strength and goodwill toward others being in the same, or worse conditions as themselves. One elder seemed more concerned about how I was doing as a Black man in Minnesota, than about his own needs. The middle-aged seemed to speak with alacrity, wanting no handouts, yet accepting what was being given with a sense that this would not last long because I'll be working soon. Most refused any kind of long-term dependency programs being thrown in their direction.

President Bush calls on Congress to rebuild

The liberals are talking about welfare programs, rebuilding with assistance that will send people back to the same conditions that have traumatized families and created crime, the same conditions that created unemployment in New Orleans.

The liberals argue against any conservative approach, such as Bush's proposal to create a ownership opportunity zone offering incentives for firms toward jobs, investment, tax relief for small businesses, and loans and loan guarantees to help businesses get up and running. Liberals have criticized this proposal as another ploy to benefit big business fostering distrust and hate toward Republican once again in communities of color.

Some folks will disagree with anything a Republican has to offer, for no other reason than it's a Republican offering the idea. From what this author has pulled together, it appears that the victims of Katrina welcome this concept of business and having jobs in their immediate neighborhoods. No more traveling outside ones neighborhood for employment. Enterprise zones in their neighborhoods. Bush's proposal is alarming to Democrats because if implanted, would break-down dependency, and would remove the victimization mentality of Blacks causing dependency on White liberals. Blacks would gain independence under the Bush plan, while White liberals would lose control.

Tell me liberals. What's wrong with Blacks in New Orleans having excellent jobs and businesses that they operate, in their community?

Liberals. Why are you afraid of Bush wanting to set up workers recovery accounts of up to $5,000 for job training and education. The liberals while giving out welfare, which keeps families down, will argue that this is chump change and will do nothing toward educating the poor toward meaningful jobs. These liberals underestimate the drive and spirit of New Orleans people that never had much of anything.

With this amount of money one could take a short medical course and once hired, use that education to build on with employee education benefits. Liberals accepting Black inferiority are afraid that Blacks will utilize benefits on the job to grow. Thus improving their quality of life. This is scary to the liberal perceptions of Black, and poor Whites. This would take away the need for liberals to act as saviors because Blacks will build from self-reliance and become empowered, thus liberal would lose the dependent voting constituent. Why would anyone stand against this concept? Because, Bush offered it and liberals fear its powerful outcome.

Bush wants to pass an urban homesteading act that offers low-income residents free building sites on federal land. I asked evacuees about this at the assistance site. Most never owned a home. Most paid their rent and by doing so, help the landlord pay his/her mortgage. If Kerry or Gore offered this concept, folks would give it adulation as if the Lord himself offered it.

Bush wants to offer 100 percent reimbursement to states to cover their costs for health care for treating many New Orleans evacuees through the end of the year. I have heard people throughout this great country say this would benefit his brother Jeb Bush. I will not comment on this inept mind set. Most of you must know that it will take money to provide for the health needs of our fellow Americans that survived Katrina? Sorry, I am obtuse because all of the evacuees are in perfect health.

I postulate that even the college liberal must agree with this one. Bush wants to offer a six-month forgiveness on student loan interests for affected areas, at an estimated cost of $100 million. The liberal must be confused. All the concepts Bush's presented toward rebuilding New Orleans seem like the liberal agenda. Bush is giving, giving, giving. Oh! The difference is giving with a concept of independence and self-reliance vs. the liberal dependency solutions.

Humphrey Job Corps Center investigation

Minnesota Lawyers are looking into allegations that Black students are being told they cannot have braids, dreads, or hair coloring on campus. The consequence. Booted out of the liberal learning facility. In this liberal organization serving young people from poor neighborhoods, potential students are refused admission because of unpaid court fines, owing child support, and other minor violations of crime. How many poor and potential students of color are refused admission because of racial profiling that gives way to unpaid traffic fines, or other police encounters?

This is a liberal facility serving poor community. Students are booted off campus for alcohol use, while some of the staff is in recovery themselves. I was taught that this behavior is reserved for Republicans. Look at liberal organizations in your areas and challenge acts of racism therein.

SAGACITY 11
WHY BROTHER KERRY LOST
THE ELECTION

The presidential election is over and time has gone by, allowing many of you an opportunity to reach catharsis, knowing we can and will continue to improve the quality of life for Black people regardless of political party.

It is my sincere belief that some of our leaders who foster dependency toward success, or doom toward defeat, because of any election outcome, have realized that we are a strong culture of Black Americans capable of saving ourselves, capable of improving our quality of life without government dependency, and not based on political affiliations but on Black individuation and self-reliance.

Kerry lost the election not because of what he said about himself, but for what he said about President Bush. On preventing another 9/11, Kerry indicated that Bush left our alliances in shatters across the globe and we are around 10 percent of casualties.

Most people understand the need to defend our basic freedoms such as school choice, choice of religion, choice to select the type of job we want and the education needed to pursue our dreams, to raise a family and freedom of speech. Because we enjoy our basic freedoms, we understand the concept of Martin Luther King's statement *"injustice anywhere is a threat to justice everywhere."* Thus it's this concept that Bush would move to protect the people of Iraq. Kerry underestimated the good will of the American people.

On whether the Iraq war makes the U.S. safer, Kerry accused Bush of failure to use superbly trained forces. Some of you such as myself, serving in any branch of the military, know that we have the best-trained military forces with respect to soldiers and equipment. This comment was a major disservice to Blacks serving in the military, which could be one reason for so many Black military troops supporting Bush.

On Bush's war plan. Kerry indicated that Bush *"rushed to war in Iraq without a plan and botched the job along the way."* This was too comical for some of the most dedicated Democrats to believe. With the influence of Powell, Rice and others, are we to believe there was no plan?

Kerry attempted to justify this inept assertion by mentioning the number of casualties weekly during his campaign. The world would accept the reality that in war, despite the best planning, we shall have casualties. To our best historians, I ask you to provide one major war in America, in Africa, in Asia, anywhere, whereby, we have not had casualties. When it came to voting, not only Republicans, but also Democrats rejected this wild assertion by Kerry.

Brother Kerry supported the war and later failed to back the troops. Brother Kerry indicated the war in Iraq was a failed war. Someone help me understand how Kerry would compare the war in Iraq to a Pottery Barn slogan about owning merchandise if one breaks it.

Brother Kerry continued to slam the troops, saying they were not trained, there was no plan Kerry made these remarks while innocent people in Iraq were being beheaded, while individuals and families were being found in mass graves. Kerry would now gain the code name "*Stupid*" hereinafter, "*Stuped.*"

This was really a good one. On homeland security, Kerry indicated Bush spent $500 million on Iraq security while cutting funding for cops and firehouses in America. Can anyone explain this to me? Why would firefighters and police throughout America support Bush if stuped's assertion is true?

If you thought the preceding paragraphs caused you emotional uneasiness, let me conclude with some medication to help you relax. Remember that show where this brother on the guitar would say, "*Wrote a song about it, like to hear it, hear it go.*" Sorry, like Brother Kerry I got lost and vacillated. Kerry stated, "*I made a mistake in how I talked about the war, but the president made a mistake in invading Iraq.*" Sounds like lyrics for Snoop Dog, Kerry.

Question: Didn't Kerry support going to war? Two plus two equals four. If one makes repeated mistakes in how one articulates the war, wouldn't one make mistakes leading the war?

Kerry indicated, "*What I worry about with the president is he's not acknowledging what's on the ground. Certainly sometimes can get you into trouble.*" How in the world could Kerry direct our nation if he can't look down and see what is under his feet?

For those of you still having pain and suffering due to Kerry not winning the election, I hope that the reasons provided will serve as some kind of therapy. If not, we have plenty of election therapy sessions to help you move on with your disorder.

I must ask this question: Look at the leaders in our community who preached doom for our people before and after the elections. The doomsday preachers all seem to be doing just fine. Those doomsday leaders didn't accept their own doomsday preaching, and you shouldn't either.

The next time someone tells you how awful it is for Blacks under Bush, look at them and ask, "Will you share with me how you're making it?"

SAGACITY 12
HOUSE REPUBLICANS IN
MINNESOTA RESPOND

✦

SPEAKER: STEVE SVIGGUM
HOUSE MAJORITY LEADER: ERIC PAULSEN

In an effort to provide the reader with "New Perspectives."

I was able to catch up with some members of the Minnesota House of Representatives—Rep. Steve Sviggum (R-Kenyon), speaker of the Minnesota House, and Rep. Erik Paulsen (R-Eden Prairie), House majority leader—and challenge them to some hard-hitting Q & A.

Q: Why should African Americans support Republicans?

Paulsen: While Democrats expect the African American vote every election, Republicans are working hard to earn African American support and don't take your votes for granted.

Colin Powell, Condoleezza Rice and Rod Paige—what do all three of these people have in common? They're all African American Republicans holding top positions in President Bush's administration. They're some of the most well-respected and powerful people in the world.

Powell, Rice and Paige, as well as many other African Americans, are Republicans because our party believes in and fights passionately for the institutions (faith, family and small business) and policies (school choice, low taxes, strong national defense) that help African Americans and all American succeed.

Q: Why does Minnesota need a constitutional amendment defining marriage as a union between one man and one woman?

Sviggum: The need for a constitutional amendment defining marriage was prompted by a recent Massachusetts Supreme Court ruling that said Massachu-

31

setts could not prohibit homosexual marriage. That same liberal, activist court then mandated the Massachusetts legislature to make same-sex marriage legal by May 17 of this year.

The concern is that the Massachusetts ruling could be used by liberal judges and politicians to undo or thwart Minnesota's law. The liberal mayor of San Francisco recently ignored California law and opened the doors of city hall for gay couples from across the country to get married. And soon, gay couples from our state married in Massachusetts will likely demand that their marriage be legally recognized in Minnesota.

The only way to stop gay marriage from coming to Minnesota is by passing a constitutional amendment. House Republicans have passed legislation that would let voters decide whether to constitutionally define marriage in Minnesota as a union between one man and one woman. But Democrats, who control the Minnesota Senate, are refusing to let Minnesotans vote on this important issue. If voters don't get a chance to weigh in on it in the upcoming election and gay marriage becomes a reality in our state, Minnesota Democrats will be directly responsible.

Q: How does President Bush's federal "No Child Left Behind" law help children of color?

Paulsen: For almost 40 years, our state has had federal funds to spend as we saw fit to help increase the performance of disadvantaged children in our classrooms. We've accomplished very little with those funds. The achievement gap between White and minority students remains wide across the country.

In Minnesota, as students enter high school, White students are functioning at the eighth grade level, where they should be, while Black students, as a group, are functioning at the level of fourth graders. That achievement gap is an embarrassment to our state. But what's even more embarrassing is the fact that our state never has been held accountable for the federal dollars we receive to address this issue.

President Bush's "No Child Left Behind" law addresses the achievement gap and helps minority students because it"

- Provides children in public schools identified as needing improvement transportation to another public school within their district.

- Provides children with tutoring when they are struggling.

- Requires consistently under performing schools to develop corrective action to ensure all children are receiving a quality education.

- Helps parents, educators and schools identify where problems exist.

- Allow parents to receive better information about how their child and their child's school are performing.

Q: Why did the Minnesota legislature pass the Personal Protection Act (commonly) referred to as "conceal-carry" last year?

Sviggum: Minnesota's had conceal-carry since 1975, but the old law needed to be changed. The law passed last year changed the state's conceal-carry law from a "may-issue" statute to a "shall-issue" statute, meaning that if you meet the requirements to obtain a permit, your county sheriff "shall-issue" you one.

We needed to change this law and create a uniform, statewide standard because the "may-issue" statute was arbitrary, unfair and discriminatory. Under the "may-issue" law, county sheriffs and city police chiefs had the sole power to issue or deny permits.

As a result, in some parts of the state, all you had to do to get a conceal-carry permit was tell the sheriff or chief you wanted one, and you got it. But in other parts of the state, mainly the metro area, your chances of obtaining a permit were about as good as winning the lottery.

Many metro sheriffs and chiefs didn't give permits to anyone under the old law, no matter how much of a personal safety concern an applicant had. That's why there are countless stories of law-abiding people who should have been granted permits under the old law but were denied, like a Minneapolis woman trained to handle a handgun whose roommate was raped and the rapist was at large, or a prison guard who was receiving threats from current and former inmates

By the way, laws allowing citizens' to carry weapons have been in effect for years in several states in America. The Wild West shootouts that Democrats predicted would happen have not come true. Liberals would foster hate toward Republicans telling us how such laws would increase Black on Black crime. It has not happened with law abiding gun carriers.

SAGACITY 13
THE BUSH TAPES

◆

BEHIND THE CURTAIN OR IN FRONT; BUSH IS THE SAME MAN

I would postulate with a snooty degree of meticulousness that many people, hearing of an author who secretly recorded his conversations with then-Gov. George Bush, might think this would be damaging to the veracity of the president after being released to the public for the world to hear. However, this has not been the outcome.

One is left with the conclusion that Bush is the same man in public that he is in private, unlike some others who will talk all kinds of stuff behind closed doors, only to later regret such inept remarks after exiting office.

Perhaps there is some truth to the myth that there are no friends in politics. This author named Doug Wead, a former aide to Bush's old man, gets an idea to write a book. Now the dude needs some attention and out breaks some really slick tape recordings between him and the president.

Many states have what is known as the one-person consent law, meaning you can record a conversation as long as you're a part of it. However, you may not record a conversation of which you are not a part. This would be sneak dropping.

Wead is clever enough to realize that releasing secret conversations between himself and the president would boost the sales of his book. In order to avoid a cheap plug, this author will not give the reader the name of the book.

In a segment of the tapes released to CNN by ABC News the president does not admit to using marijuana and responds, "*But you got to understand, I want to be president, I want to lead. I want to set—do you want your little kid to say 'Hey, Daddy, President Bush tried some marijuana, I think I will?'*"

The fact is, parents are observed by their children using drugs; this would be more of acquiescence, in my opinion. Nevertheless, Bush's answer, unknowingly

34

being recorded, is unswerving compared to his position on liberty and freedom and his answer regarding drug use throughout his campaign and during his presidency.

This president would admit to an alcohol problem. This matter was resolved through the cleansing of Jesus Christ, as he has admitted repeatedly.

The president did not admit to the use of cocaine. I have this attitude about not capitulating by responding to rumors. Likewise, Bush has developed an association with truth and is not moved to respond to untruths.

The Christian is not compelled to respond to lies. Is this not the example Jesus Christ provided us? Being the spiritual outcome, Bush responded to reports of alcohol abuse as being true. Yet, his cocaine response, which has dogged him since the 2000 election, is very different.

"*The cocaine thing let me tell you my strategy on that*" Bush said on the tape. "*Rather than saying no…I think it's time for someone to draw the line and look people in the eye and say, you know, I'm not going to participate in ugly rumor about me and blame my opponent, and hold the line. Stand up for a system that will not allow for this kind of crap to go on.*"

How many times do we read in scripture whereby, Jesus Christ promulgated the same message? Here, we witness Bush in public, as in this unknowingly recorded conversation with the Wead.

Bush also corrected the Wead when he said that an evangelical leader had said Bush promised not to hire gay men and lesbians. This reminds me of President Wilson. Wilson fired all the Black federal workers and replaced them with White Southern Democrats.

Bush response: "*No, what I said was I wouldn't fire gays.*" He goes on, "*I'm not going to discriminate against people.*" By the way, did you know Bush has more people of color and women in high levels within his cabinet than any other president, including the Bill Clinton.

One will have to hate Bush for a few other things—being a Republican, becoming a millionaire, the governor of Texas, and the president of the United States. Any other reason is ludicrous.

SAGACITY 14
A VOTE AGAINST CARRYING GUNS IS A VOTE AGAINST BLACK EQUALITY

I have trained a lot of Asians, Whites, and Hispanics in my permit-to-carry class, and only a handful of Blacks, more women than to men. Slavery is over. It's all right to carry a gun legally.

The Black Panthers were the first group of Black men and women to free themselves of the fear pushed on us after of Reconstruction by liberal Southerners and the Ku Klux Klan that former slaves will not take up weapons. I call this act the psychological ramifications of the hooded ones ordering Blacks not to have weapons or else.

Owning a weapon and carrying a weapon, as a law-abiding Black person is a part of our civil rights. To those brothers and sisters who have your permits to carry, as the brother on the Mod Squad would say, *"Solid."*

Democrats' "no" votes denied Blacks equal opportunity

History shall show, without any doubt, that throughout America, permits to carry guns were not issued to people of color equally when compared to Whites and/or family members of law enforcement officials. The new permit-to-carry law provides equal access to law-abiding Blacks who complete the required training.

For once, with respect to carrying weapons, we are equal. The spirit of each Black Panther member must be joyful. Knowing this how could any Democrat vote against this basic freedom for Black people?

Blacks and Whites have died for freedom and equality. Because Blacks have been discriminated against with respect to obtaining permits-to-carry a gun, and because the new laws provides an equal playing field consistent with the civil rights theme, any liberal voting against such a law in your areas was also voting against your civil rights.

Below are the names of Democrats voting against this equality for Blacks, women, and other people of color in Minnesota.

Senate Democrats voting "no": Anderson (St. Paul), Berglin (Minneapolis), Betzold (Fridley), Chaudhary (Fridley), Cohen (St. Paul), Dibble (Minneapolis), Foley (Coon Rapids), Higgins (Minneapolis), Hottinger (St. Peter), Kelley (Hopkins), Marko (Cottage Grove), Marty (Roseville), Moua (St. Paul), Pappas (St. Paul), Pogemiller (Minneapolis), Ranum (Minneapolis), Rest (New Hope), Skoglund (Minneapolis), Solon (Duluth).

House Members voting "no": Atkins (Inver Grove Heights), Bernardy (Fridley), Biernat (Minneapolis), Carlson (Crystal), Clark, K. (Minneapolis), Davnie (Minneapolis), Dorn (Mankato), Ellison (Minneapolis), Entenza (St. Paul), Goodwin (Columbia Heights), Greiling (Roseville), Hausman (St. Paul), Hillstrom (Brooklyn Center), Hilty (Finlayson), Hornstein (Minneapolis), Huntley (Duluth), Jaros (Duluth), Johnson, S. (St. Paul), Kahn (Minneapolis), Kelliher (Minneapolis), Larson (Bloomington), Latz (St. Louis Park), Lenczewski (Bloomington), Lesch (St. Paul), Mahoney (St. Paul), Mariani (St. Paul), Mullery (Minneapolis), Nelson, M. (Brooklyn Park), Opatz (St. Cloud), Otto (May Township), Paymar (St. Paul), Pelowski (Winona), Peterson (Madison), Pugh (South St. Paul), Sieben (Newport), Slawick (Maplewood), Thao (St. Paul), Thissen (Minneapolis), Wagenius (Minneapolis), Walker (Minneapolis), Wasiluk (Maplewood).

I am asking you to locate and identify all liberal politicians that voted against your legal right to carry a gun in your areas. These people deserve heavy scrutiny.

Republican Secretary of State working for your voting rights

Secretary of State Mary Kiffmeyer (Minnesota) has spearheaded efforts to increase voter turnout by making it easier for military voters and students abroad to cast absentee ballots.

She initiated the printing of election materials in languages other that English—Somali, Spanish, Hmong, Vietnamese, and others—something that did not exist before. She has addressed dozens of diverse community groups to promote voting and educate new voters about the election process.

The office prints several very popular voter education brochures—none existed before Secretary Kiffmeyer came into office. The office has done several videos for distribution to cable TV and to schools to promote voting and to educate voters on how to register and vote.

I share with you the outstanding work of a Republican official from Minnesota. Challenge the liberal Secretary in your state to follow Kiffmeyer's lead and make it easier for all people to vote.

Sagacity 15
Commercials targeting Blacks in the liberal media

For any Black person to smoke around their loved ones, knowing the risk of secondhand smoke, the risk of lung cancer and many other cancers, including mouth, voice box, esophagus, bladder, kidney, pancreas, liver, cervix, stomach, colon, and rectum cancers (all according to American Cancer Society), Black folks have to be weak-minded to continue the use of this poison.

Let's add the excessive use of illegal drugs, alcohol, pork and other unhealthy foods, and Black people smoking are already dead. You are spiritually dead; you are weak-minded. Resurrect your spirit, Black people. Bring your spirit back to life before it's too late. Start a campaign that will challenge liberal businesses in your neighborhoods providing cancer sticks to young people under age.

Release the grip of that evil demon targeting you through advertisements to smoke. Our Black youths as young as 13 years of age are smoking cigars, using drugs, alcohol, living unhealthy diets—they are already dead. Many of these products killing our people are sold from liberal businesses in your neighborhoods.

If you knew that within 20 minutes of your last cigarette that your heart rate would drop and your heart attack rate increase, would you continue to smoke? Will you continue to hurt yourself and your loved ones with secondhand smoke? If your answer is yes, then you are a weak-minded Black person falling victim to the many advertisements on liberal television.

If you want to stop smoking than I am going to ask you to remind yourself of how precious you are as a Black person. Your mind is precious, your heart is precious, your spirit is precious, and your body is precious. If you can accept all this preciousness, begin a process to destroy that evil demon killing your precious Black spirit. Tell a friend to protest those liberal businesses in your area selling tobacco products, and alcohol that steals, kills and destroys babies, mothers, fathers and families in your neighborhoods.

Black folks in the gym

I have been in the gym all year. Heck! Once again, the gyms are saturated with Black trying to get into shape. I tell other committed people, now waiting nervously for equipment, *"Don't worry, in 30 days, or less, these people will be gone."*

They seem to be like some kind of Gym-Gone product. How in the world can you expect that after doing nothing the summer before, now in the gym, after all winter of doing nothing, you are going to whip that unsightly body into something a woman or man will want to observe

Prepare for the 300-meter run by sprinting as fast as you can for one-minute periods. A one and one-half mile run (16 minutes, 15 seconds) requires a good level of cardiovascular fitness. This requires 25-40 minutes of cardiovascular exercise four to five times a week.

Exert yourself to a level equal to about 70 percent of your target heart rate. Bench press must equal 102 lbs. or 60 percent of your body weight. Heck! This is already a problem for some of you every-now-and-then gym buffs.

To continue: This requires bicep, triceps, and chest strength. Work with free weights or machines doing military press, bicep curls, triceps extensions, bench press and rows. Don't let me scare you, but work yourself up to 80 pushups within one-minute.

Don't you in-the-gym-now, out-in-three-weeks people stop reading. I have more—leg press 300 lbs. This requires strength in your lower body using machines or free weights on exercises such as squats, leg extensions, leg curls, lunges, leg press, and dead lifts. Now we have the "oh no, I can't do it" sit-ups. Yes, in just three weeks, after months of doing nothing, you to can develop the endurance in the abdominal area to obtain that tight stomach, cuts, and definition by doing several sets of abdominal exercises, such as curl-ups, crunches or sit-ups four to five times per week.

Get busy and attempt to accomplish my program by the end of the month. If you are lost, just ask any Black person who has been in the gym on an ongoing schedule. My program works for liberal as well. Just joking here.

SAGACITY 16
MINNESOTA'S PARTY'S
EXECUTIVE DIRECTOR DUCKS
RACE QUESTION

We submitted the following letter to Cory Miltimore, the executive director of the Minnesota Republican Party:

July 13, 2004

Sir,

We started the Minnesota Black Republican Coalition in the year 2000. The name was appropriate at the time. We have accomplished our goals under that accepted name. Now you must benefit from our accomplishments by taking bold action based on the symbol and strategy having been established by President Bush.

Let me explain.

President Bush does not refer to his top cabinet members as Black this, or Black that. President Bush has captured the hearts of all America by placing people that look like America in top paid positions. Therefore, if you are to benefit from our labor, you too, sir, must place Blacks in positions of pay throughout the Republican Party main offices and other locations within the party.

The name Black Republican Coalition is not inclusive. We have reached out to various cultures desiring to be a part of our mission. The name has served its purpose and is now archaic. We find Urban Republican more inclusive. President Bush has never referred to his key advisors as Black. This is obvious.

Follow the courage, the wisdom and the leadership of our President. Change the face of the party starting in your office and throughout the Republican

Party—in key paid visible positions. President Bush's actions are the real solution.

Should you have the character of our President? Make the changes herein requested. Not to do so shall bring into question the image of our Republican Party of Minnesota and its real commitment to being inclusive—thus destroying the work of House and Senate members and others that have accomplished so much over the years.

The time is now. It is a terrible feeling to hear people continue to tell me that they see no Blacks in the main office and/or other key areas in paid positions. Should this not change, our work shall become breathless and die.

Cc: President Bush
United States of America

The Response from Mr. Miltimore failed to address the specifics of our letter. Therefore, we made a decision not to provide that response. Our next question to Mr. Miltimore: What are your plans to utilize the Black press in your efforts toward reaching out to communities of color? We hope for a more direct response.

You, the reader have witnessed our challenge to Republican leadership. All have responded honestly, and with enthusiasm. Our intent is not to cast a shadow on other Republican leaders. This is an isolated failure to respond by Mr. Miltimore. Perhaps because he had nothing concrete by which to offer?

Challenge your political leadership. Challenge them to show your community members their commitment by what they have accomplished, not by what those leaders expect to accomplish. Challenge the Democrat, the liberal leadership to move beyond talk and our impasse regarding matters of concern. This would take a lot of courage if you're a Black liberal to challenge liberal leadership within your communities. If you do so, you may discover you are more conservative in ideology than expected.

SAGACITY 17
CONTROVERSY

To show my appreciation for you reading the most controversial book about liberal racism anywhere, I am offering you an opportunity to be featured in our column in the Minnesota Spokesman-Recorder Newspaper. Respond in 200 words or less to questions presented. If selected, your responses will be provided in my column.

As a Black person, which are you more worried about: the Patriot Act, the recent Supreme Court ruling regarding eminent domain? Remember, the most controversial response will appear in our column. Send your response to mnbrc@hotmail.com

Liberal racism has commendable company

I am happy to observe an increased number of Black men and women seeking permits to carry guns in the United States. Far too long those liberals have opposed Blacks' second amendment right to have weapons. Now, for the first time law enforcement cannot discriminate when issuing permits to carry a pistol because of many states licensed to carry laws.

The new law mandates the issuance of permits to carry upon successfully completing a training course from a certified instructor. For those liberal politicians and others who opposed this law, you are in good company with other gun control advocates including Adolph Hitler, Joseph Stalin, V.L. Lenin and the Ku Klux Klan.

Liberals filibustered anti-lynching laws

Did you know that the Democrats filibustered anti-lynching and civil rights laws that Republicans work hard to push through the walls of congress?

Big lips, big eyes and Black

Jesse Jackson and others have been protesting a stamp flowing around in Mexico depicting out-of-the-ordinary Negro features. Hey, what about Speedy Gonzales?

Understanding the Black Conservative and our Purpose

"To work realistically using collective wisdom to support the election and re-election of public office holders who share our vision and work to promote the principle of limited government in public life, with commitment to affirmative access as defined by President Bush allowing an equal playing field for all law-abiding, hard-working, non-excuse-making people of color.

"We commit ourselves to promoting the sanctity of human life, choice of education, economic self-empowerment, and working toward the elimination of long-term dependency programs that have destroyed the Black family while maintaining a commitment toward strong, workable, affirmative access policies. To work toward a strong moral climate, freedom through limited government, USA Black Conservative Committee will continue to advocate our goals and objectives through media campaigns and shall provide quantitative and qualitative analysis on relevant issues of importance to the Black community.

"Through these actions, with measurable outcomes, we shall promote the tenets of democracy and political action giving Black Christians and others a voice in government. When other community organizations fail, are at an impasse, have lost credibility, or are afraid to represent you, we will stand up with collective wisdom, honor and integrity. We shall be there!"

Jobs for youth

Youths ages 16-24, are you interested in helping elect Republican candidates? Want to get involved in grassroots politics? This would be a great way to learn about conservative politics.

It's possible that you can use this experience toward school credits. This is a perfect opportunity for students interested in a short-term or part-time evening/weekend jobs. If you're interested call the local Republican office in your area.

SAGACITY 18
MINNESOTA HOUSE HONORS
SLAVES WHO BUILT U.S.
CAPITOL

◆

I AM ASKING YOU TO GET YOUR HOUSE MEMBERS TO DO THE SAME IN YOUR STATE.

A statement from Minnesota State Representative Erick Paulsen:

"I was pleased to sponsor the House resolution honoring slaves who built the U.S. Capitol as a small but important symbol of Minnesota's gratitude to those who worked so hard to build this important monument to freedom. Through his work tracing the history of Black slave labor and the construction of the U.S. Capitol, Lucky Rosenbloom has taught members of the House an important lesson during Black History month."

We got it done on the state level. The Minnesota House passed a resolution Monday, February 16, in honor of Black History Month, recognizing slave laborers who helped build the U.S. Capitol.

"Families were sold and separated, children were born never knowing their father or their mother, and people were born into a society where they were considered property," said House Majority Leader Paulsen of Eden Prairie. "The only thing that those individuals had in their life was their spirit."

Minnesota Black Republican Coalition President Lucky Rosenbloom spearheaded the resolution. A similar measure proposed in the U.S. Congress would go a step further, establishing a commission to recommend an appropriate memorial to the slaves who helped build the Capitol.

The Minnesota House Resolution reads:

A house resolution honoring the slave laborers who worked on the construction of the United States Capitol

WHEREAS, the United States Capitol stands as a symbol of democracy, equality, and freedom to the entire world; and

WHEREAS, the year 2004 marks the 204th anniversary of the opening of this historic structure for the first session of Congress to be held in the new capital city; and

WHEREAS, slavery was not prohibited throughout the United States until the ratification of the 13th amendment to the Constitution in 1865; and

WHEREAS, prior to that date, African American slave labor was both legal and common in the District of Columbia and the adjoining states of Maryland and Virginia; and

WHEREAS, public records attest to the fact that African American slave labor was used in the construction of the United States Capitol; and

WHEREAS, public records further attest to the fact that the five dollar per month payment for African American slave labor was made to the slave owners and not to the laborer; and

WHEREAS, African Americans made significant contributions and fought bravely for freedom during the American Revolutionary War;

NOW, THEREFORE, BE IT RESOLVED by the Committee on Rules and Legislative Administration of the House of Representatives of the States of Minnesota that it recognizes and honors the contributions of those African American slaves whose efforts helped to build the United States Capitol. It expresses its appreciation for the time, the labor, and skills they gave to the creation of this monument to freedom, even while they were not free. (January 21, 2004)

U.S. Senator Coleman cosponsors resolution in congress to recognize slaves

Lucky Rosenbloom and Urban Youth have been working since 2001 to get slaves recognized that helped build the U.S. Capitol. Below are comments from Sen. Coleman regarding the Resolution introduced into Congress.

"I am a proud cosponsor of a Senate Resolution to create a Congressional task force to officially document the contributions of African American slaves in constructing the U.S. Capitol. While the great tragedy of slave labor being used to construct one of the world's great symbols of freedom of the world can never be fully addressed, I am hopeful that we can do something to recognize the tremendous historical contributions of these American citizens to our history. This legislation is just a small part of our never-ending obligation to find healing for an era of immense pain and suffering. The representatives of American freedom, working in a house of the greatest Democracy the world has ever seen, have a responsibility to honor the memories and contributions of those that built it without their own liberty intact."

We hope that you, the reader, will offer your support as we move this issue for national recognition. Write in your support to: USA Black Conservative Committee. P.O. Box 4171, St. Paul, MN 55104. Contact your U.S. Senator and ask him/her if they know of this resolution and if he/she is supporting this worthy cause?

SAGACITY 19
LIBERALS FIGHT THE STAND
YOUR GROUND BILL

Lawmakers in the U.S. state of Florida have passed a bill that would allow a gun owner to shoot an attacker on the street in self-defense. Don't you think we need this law in Minnesota?

Under what its Republican sponsor calls the Stand Your Ground bill, gun license holders over 21 years of age who feel threatened in public can shoot to protect themselves, without trying to escape first. Oh no! Some of you are against this law because of a Republican originating the law. Hang on.

Liberal Democrats, while living in areas they forbid you to move into, don't have to worry as we do. Democrats want you to be Bible-carrying victims. What is wrong with having the ability to protect yourself and laws that benefit you instead of more laws that protect the criminals?

Florida Governor Jeb Bush says the bill is a good anti-crime measure and this author agrees. It's time we make the criminal feel unsafe on the streets. Now, it's the other way around. Law-abiding people are afraid to be on the streets. We must shift this around my friends.

Critics say it will boost gun sales and turn the state into something resembling the Wild West. I recall the liberals promoting that Blacks would go crazy and shoot each other in mad numbers before the permit-to-carry law was passed in Minnesota. We continue to have thugs killing each other, yet not one Black person with a permit to carry has used his/her weapon illegally in Minnesota.

The law has been framed liberals as a "shoot to kill" law. It is not. There is no new license to use deadly force. Anyone that would be licensed to carry a gun would be required to use retreat as the first option.

The law is very clear about when deadly force can be used. I would have to be directly threatened. I cannot shoot to prevent an auto theft, for instance.

The law basically removes the civil and criminal liability for the lawful use of a firearm in self-defense. Unfortunately, there had been lawsuits by convicted felons against law-abiding citizens for the use of a firearm in self-defense. And the criminals were winning.

This is a terrible act by the criminal, bringing legal action against an innocent person.

Currently, the criminals have more rights than you, the law-abiding, hard-working American. To have a law such as this in your state would allow you to protect yourselves against predatory criminals without fear of these thugs bringing civil action against the innocent. Here is how I view the matter: I am still required under law to take every possible action to prevent and avoid the use of deadly force. Should I be forced to protect myself and/or family from great bodily harm, or death, the law would offer protection by allowing a response at a higher degree of force to prevent an attack. Contact your legislators and work for such a law in your area.

A question for liberal critics

Since liberal critics are hysterically opposed to law-abiding citizens being given the right to defend themselves against criminals. Will these liberals support, and will your legislature provide funding for more police officers to protect the citizens on your block, in your home, in parking lots, on your way to the store, in your yard, or simply out for a walk?

Americans must be allowed to use deadly force in a public place if they have a reasonable belief they are in danger of death or great bodily harm. It applies to all means of force that may result in death, being threatened by someone with a bat, knife, or any other weapon that would produce substantial, great bodily harm or death. If you are attacked, you should not have to retreat.

Most liberals have few objections allowing people to protect themselves from intruders in their homes, but say the provision making it easier to use deadly force in public gives gun owners a license to kill. However, liberals want you to believe that this law could lead to racially motivated killings and Black on Black crime. This argument suggests that Black people are not civilized..

SAGACITY 20
SLAVE RECOGNITION MOVING FORWARD

S.Con.Res17 [recognition of slave laborers on U.S. Capitol] remains on the table. The reason this must move forward is because 246 years of an enterprise murderous of both the people and their culture is so unprecedentedly massive that it would require some form of collective blindness not to see it and, during slavery, its living victims. This recognition shall continue to honor not only the slaves, but also all people who have struggled and died for freedom, equality and civil rights. I repeat this because of the importance of this recognition. Call your U.S. Senator and ascertain if he/she has knowledge of this resolution.

Statement from U.S. Senator Norm Coleman

"While the great tragedy of slave labor being used to construct one of the world's greatest symbols of freedom in the world can never be fully addressed, I am hopeful that we can do something to recognize the historical contributions of these American citizens to our history.

"These tremendous individuals helped lay down the actual foundation of our democracy. I am pleased that Senate Report 108-307 to the Senate Legislative Branch Appropriations bill for fiscal year 2005 (S.2666) includes language directing the architect of the capitol, working with the historians of the Senate and House and the librarian of Congress, to study the history and contributions of slave laborers in construction of the U.S. Capitol, and provide a report to Congress within 180 days of enactment.

"In July, I sent a letter to Senator Ben Nighthorse Campbell, chairman of the Senate Subcommittee on Legislative Branch Appropriations, expressing my support for efforts to recognize the contributions of slave laborers in the construction of the U.S. Capitol. I expect the Legislative Branch Appropriations bill for fiscal year 2005 to be considered on the Senate Floor very soon, possibly as early as next week."

Sen. Coleman's intellect and courage toward getting a recognition for African American slaves who helped build the U.S. Capitol continues to bring life to the spirits of so many people, including women, Blacks, Whites and others, who throughout history have given their lives toward the themes of freedom, equality and justice. Knowing Sen. Coleman is working toward this recognition is comforting.

Contact your U.S. Senator of your area and ask him/her the status of this Resolution. We must keep this recognition alive.

SAGACITY 21
THE ADDICTED ELDERLY—A GROWING CONCERN

I wanted to share my interview, which springs from my discussions with a 58-year-old subject who began using alcohol and cocaine in a nightclub in the city of Minneapolis. The subject used these chemicals for years, keeping the use a secret from his family members.

In talking with my subject, I learned that his secret of chemical use was made known to his family when he was jailed for possession of cocaine and an open bottle after a traffic violation minor in nature. The subject is now in treatment and confesses that it took him years to admit that he has a problem with chemicals.

While my study regarding Rule 25 is focused on my subject, it is with intent that I shift to a perspective of a larger population of black elderly people. My subject is but one of a growing group of elderly people who abuse drugs such as alcohol, cocaine, marijuana, and, perhaps to the reader's surprise, heroin. As elderly people live longer, become more isolated, internalize oppression, fears, financial problems and depression; the number of elderly addicts will continue to grow.

My subject has a Master's Degree and is very articulate and extremely intelligent despite his troubles with chemicals. He and other middle-class elderly feel as though the system does not recognize their problems. The Rule 25 is developed with little thought given to Black elderly people.

The police and courts will often let an elderly person go when in possession of illegal drugs. Conversely, if a young person is arrested, he/she is allowed to proceed through the system. The young offender is brought before a chemical assessor, evaluated, and offered help. Elderly people often will not get help unless they are made to do so.

Any good assessor, trained to work with seniors, could get that senior appropriate help. This presents the issue for seniors who are released from the jurisdiction of the courts and not mandated to have the Rule 25 assessment. At issue is whether an elderly person should be considered a specific class with special treatment when arrested and/or tagged for drug use or possession.

My prognosis using education, street smarts, and experience in talking with my elderly subject and young people is that the road to illegal chemical and/or legal chemical use among the elderly is varied. The combination of street drugs and prescription drugs may all be ways of coping with feelings of uselessness, isolation, medical problems, and fear of being victims of crime.

It's the mixture of these drugs that is such a danger to our seniors. Young users of yesterday become elderly users of today. The people who used drugs in the '50s and '60s are adding to the growing number of addicted elderly.

Imagine the strains associated with hypertension, lupus, diabetes and other medical concerns unique to the elderly. Chemicals and drugs add to the risk of heart attacks and add pressure to the brain that the elderly cannot handle. The elderly are made up of different races, ages, sexes and economic status. Perhaps the common factors are that they are seniors by age group and that most have or will soon develop medical concerns during continuous use of chemicals.

In terms of standards of chemical use applied in a Rule 25 assessment, they may not focus on the needs of the elderly in that their reasons for using may not be the same as the reasons at an earlier age. Therefore, issues that may have been of assistance to an assessor in the past may not be in the present.

For example, if a senior is isolated he/she will not spend time with friends who will glamorize the use of chemicals. The elderly may not suffer financially due to chemical use as he/she did at a younger age. Thus, in a Rule 25 assessment with respect to Black elderly, assumptions are made and realistic episodic factors such as seasonal depressions associated with chemical use maybe overlooked.

The impact of chemical use in the elderly population is no doubt a lot higher than we might expect. As it relates to African-Americans and other elders of color, the impact is greater as they are often denied access to services, thereby creating more anxiety and a need for relief with chemicals. Types of chemical dependency services needed are AA groups focusing on elders of color. Perhaps multicultural groups would be acceptable, but only if a racial balance has been created.

I hope these observations may provide those working with the elderly an added perspective, or help raise new issues relevant to the elderly and chemical use. If as an assessor you are able to more closely examine your use of the Rule 25 in relations to the elderly of color, or if the courts would look at elderly abusers as seriously as they do the young abuser, we can begin a new process of identifying and finding solutions to the often unknown or hidden problems of the elderly and the growth in their chemical use.

SAGACITY 22
POLICE ACCUSED OF MISCONDUCT: AN OFFICER RESPONDS

Once a police officer has been accused of wrongdoing, does he/she really ever loose the stain of that accusation? Probably not! Why? Because the police officer is employed by a political structure called the police department. Within that structure are those who have aspirations of promotion, and they are won and lost by whom you align yourself with.

Even if the accusation has been proven false, you nonetheless might be labeled brash, flashy, or a loose cannon, and no aspirer can afford to be associated with you. You may be a promotional leper and not know it.

The police department has its political counterpart, called the city government. Of course, whatever the police might do may reflect on city government. If an officer's name hits the news and he/she is accused of a wrongdoing, city government may want that problem to go away, or at the very least be kept in its place.

This means that the police officer is unofficially labeled non-promotable and/or a political liability. Because of a malicious lie or to even out a vendetta, a police officer's integrity is permanently impugned and always subject to further speculations because of the news media's eagerness to jump on a story. The following is one officer's perspective on this issue.

"I've been working in North Minneapolis for the past seven years as a street cop. I've never met you [Lucky], but I have heard good things about you from other officers. Regarding your questions about officers being unfairly accused by criminals, it has a significant emotional effect on all officers.

"The Steven Porter non-incident has quietly faded away since it became apparent that the whole thing was fabricated by a habitual criminal looking for sympathy, and trying to avoid a long prison sentence.

"As a white officer working a primarily Black sector of the North Side, I've always been notified of complaints where the arrested person has alleged that I used the 'N'-word. Lucky, the idea that officers are risking this secure job by randomly throwing out racial slurs is foolish and self-defeating. If officers truly harbored the rage against minorities, which some people (and publications) have alleged, the number of documented violations would be enormous!

"Even without documentation or any credibility on the accuser's part, officers are still being paraded down t o the Civilian Review Authority to try to explain why they didn't say what they are accused of saying. It's difficult to allege that the police beat you when you have no injuries to display, but racial slurs are easy to claim and difficult to disprove, especially when two or three allegations occur within a short period of time by felons facing extensive prison sentences.

"The word 'aggressive' has fallen out of favor with many of our liberal counterparts, but I'm not ashamed to say that most North Side officers aggressively perform their job as police officers. With a spike in homicides and more gangs and guns than ever before, officers have to be careful when dealing with known gang members in hostile locations.

"Being aggressive and acting instead of reacting are elements which keep officers and law abiding citizens safe from the habitual criminals who are booked and released in an endless cycle. Law-abiding citizens who harbor no ill will toward police officers probably want an aggressive officer looking for the person who violated them and turned them into a victim.

"Lucky, there are too many good, hard-working, law-abiding citizens in North Minneapolis who would be further victimized by thugs if officers lessened there aggressive approach to dealing with these well-known predators. As a fellow Republican, I thank you for your courage in standing up to the 'mouths' who really represent no one (except themselves and a few well-known thugs)."

Here, I challenge the reader to solicit Police response to incidents of misconduct in your own cities. The liberal sees misconduct in terms of race and racial profiling. While these types of misconduct exist, the Black conservative desires strong enforcement of laws and protection of Black citizens in high crime neighborhoods. The Black conservative separates perception vs. reality of Police misconduct. Analyze the officer's response for yourself. Allow a means for officers to respond to incidents in your neighborhoods. It will improve police community relations.

SAGACITY 23
RADICAL REPUBLICANS
CLASHED WITH LINCOLN

History has documented the Ku Klux Klan platform calling for the murders of Negroes and Republicans. We work in the spirit of our courageous founders. We owe it to the spirit of a lot of people in our party to work boldly towards the elimination of hate.

I am proud to be a conservative and walk in the spirit of God and early Republicans. Let us pick up the courage of these people and come back to the party of bold leadership and change.

Some members of the Republican Party were not only in favor of the abolition of slavery, but believed that freed slaves should have complete equality with White citizens. They also opposed the Fugitive Slave Act and the Kansas-Nebraska Act. This group became known as Radical Republicans; its members included Thaddeus Stevens, Charles Sumner, Lyman Trumbull, Hannibal Hamlin, James F. Wilson, Henry Wilson, Benjamin Wade, Horace Greeley, James Garfield, Wendell Phillips and Fredrick Douglass.

After the 1860 elections, the Radical Republicans became a powerful force in Congress. Radical Republicans were critical of Abraham Lincoln during the Civil War when he was slow to support the recruitment of Black soldiers into the Union Army. Radical Republicans also clashed with Lincoln over his treatment of Major General John C. Fremont.

On August 30, 1861, Fremont, the commander of the Union Army in St. Louis, proclaimed that all slaves owned by Confederates in Missouri were free. Lincoln was furious when he heard the news, as he feared that this action would force slave owners in Border States to join the Confederate Army. Lincoln asked Fremont to modify his order and free only slaves owned by Missourians actively working for the South.

When Fremont refused, he was sacked and replaced by the conservative General Henry Halleck. The chairman of the Senate Finance Committee, William

Fessenden, described Lincoln's actions as "a weak and unjustifiable concession in the Union men of the border states." Charles Sumner wrote to Lincoln complaining about his actions and remarked how sad it was "to have the power of a god and not use it godlike."

The situation was repeated in May 1862, when General David Hunter began enlisting Black soldiers in the occupied district under his control. Soon afterwards, Hunter issued a statement that all slaves owned by Confederates in his area (Georgia, Florida, and South Carolina) were free. Lincoln was furious, and despite the pleas of Salmon Chase, the Secretary of the Treasury, he instructed him to disband the 1st South Carolina (African Descent) regiment and retract his proclamation.

In the early stages of the American Civil War, Lincoln only had one senior member of his government, Salmon Chase (secretary of the treasury), who was sympathetic to the views of the Radical Republicans. Later in the war, other radicals such as Edwin M. Stanton (secretary of war), William Fessenden (secretary of the treasury) and James Speed (attorney general) were recruited into his cabinet.

Radical Republicans were also critical of Lincoln's Reconstruction Plan. In 1862, Benjamin Wade and Henry Winter Davis sponsored a bill that provided for the administration of the affairs of Southern states by provisional governors until the end of the war. They argued that civil government should only be established when half of the male White citizens took an oath of loyalty to the Union. The Wade-Davis Bill was passed on July 2, 1864, but Abraham Lincoln refused to sign it.

Despite their insistence that the White power structure in the South should be removed, most Radical Republicans argued that the defeated forces should be treated leniently. Even while the American Civil War was going on, Charles Sumner argued, "A humane and civilized people cannot suddenly become inhumane and uncivilized. We cannot be cruel, or barbarous, or savage, because the Rebels we now meet in warfare are cruel, barbarous and savage. We cannot imitate the detested example."

After the war, Horace Greeley advocated universal amnesty and actually put up the bail for his long-term enemy, Jefferson Davis. Lyman Trumball and Hannibal Hamlin campaigned for better treatment of those Confederate leaders still in prison, and James F. Wilson took up the case of the former vice-president, Alexander Stephens.

The Radical Republicans' campaign for equal rights for African Americans was not a popular cause after the American Civil War. In 1868, Henry Wilson argued that the issue cost the Republican Party over a quarter of a million votes.

In the election that year, several of the radicals lost their seats, including the long-term leader of the group Benjamin Wade.

A social Studies teacher, I enjoy teaching youth about these radical Republicans. By the time they reach my tenth grade class, it is not surprising that may of them have no knowledge of this history because the liberal schools system and teachers fail to provide this historical education. However, it is clear that most have learned that Republicans hate them, have no concerns about their issues and were historically against civil rights. This type of fostering of hate toward Republicans is wrong and you a parent must demand that your son/daughter teachers provide the good and bad of both political parties relevant to slavery and civil rights. It has not been one sided.

SAGACITY 24
WAS CLINTON REALLY BLACK AMERICA'S FRIEND?

In his first term, former President Clinton's policies followed a distinct slant toward a more conservative and Republican course on social issues. He sponsored the most punitive crime bill in history, which passed in 1993. After suffering the defeat of his "economic stimulus package," which contained funding for urban development, he never put it back on the table.

But wait, there is more from this great Democrat who is said to be a friend to the poor and/or people of color. Clinton signed the most punitive welfare reform bill in history, which victimized Black mothers.

If President Bush, today, would do the same things, Blacks, poor people, and other minority groups would be yelling racism. They would be calling him a president who does not care about the working people, only the rich. When Clinton and other Democrats do the above-mentioned, they maintain their grip on the Black, poor Whites, and other minority groups by praying with them in our churches. Yet, let President Bush go to a Black, poor White, and/or other minority church, and there are those that would yell tricks, manipulation, and perhaps in the same sentence a few expletives. Why is this?

Stop blaming the Republicans for local problems in your community. The Republicans are not representing our community in city government and/or on a state level. Remember, you continue to elect Democrats. Yet, I hear people complaining about the same social issues over and over.

The Democrats have had a strong hold on our communities for a long time. Yet, we have also been complaining about the same things for a long time. Maybe it is time to change. It's time to start thinking conservative, to look at the Republicans and our agenda.

We have a younger generation of voters who are not feeding into this poor Democratic reproduction of dependency, Affirmative Action, or preferences that suggest we are inferior.

To reject these inferior innovations is to recognize self-reliance and individuation. Liberals don't want this self-reliance, this individuation because it threatens the base of there voting constituency which is founded on government dependency and liberal repentance.

Don't read this question!

Now that your curiosity has gotten the best of you, answer the following: If Martin Luther King, Jr. were alive today, do you really think he would advocate the killing of unborn babies?

If Malcolm X were alive today, do you think he would approve of or advocate handing out condoms in schools? Didn't brother Malcolm tell our Black women to get off welfare and work?

Do you think that these men, if alive today, would want our women on welfare, or would they prefer a people fighting for equality so that they could have meaningful jobs. Would these two men want us fighting to maintain a welfare system that keeps women oppressed and subjugated?

Why is it that when a Democrat is president people beg for more money, but when a Republican is president they beg, "Don't take our money."

Martin Luther King was a registered Republican in 1956 when the majority of Blacks were in fact Republican. Kings registration records can be found in the archives of Atlanta, Georgia. This will shock many liberals, however, is easily apprehended by the Black conservative.

Understanding the Black conservative on issues

Black conservatives support school choice, in all its forms: vouchers, charter schools, public-private alliances, and home schooling. Given that education has been the traditional path toward upward mobility for Americans, high-quality education must not be limited to those with access to financial resources. The future of our nation rests on the skills and education of today's youths. Making education a free-market system will increase competition and force educational institutions to raise current standards.

Empowerment/Enterprise Zones

Black conservatives support legislation at all levels of government that will provide tax cuts and other financial incentives for entrepreneurs and businesses to jump-start and/or relocate to underdeveloped, often neglected urban and rural areas.

Pro-life advocacy

Black conservatives believe that all human life is sacred. Human life in the womb is no different than human life outside of the womb. I support all efforts to save the lives of the unborn. I support candidates who share my commitment to this principle, especially those candidates who support parental notification, agree with the prohibition of government-funded abortions, and stand in absolute opposition to partial-birth abortions.

Social Security reform

Black conservatives promote legislation that will reform the current Social Security system through the creation of private investment saving accounts. Privatization will create more opportunities, economic development, and greater wealth for all Americans. The current system is unsound, but what is most troubling about the current system is its disproportionately detrimental effect on African American families, especially African American males. I work to educate the American people and reform Social Security to increase and ensure economic stability, security and opportunity for all generations.

SAGACITY 25
THE CONCLUSION
SLAVES TO BE RECOGNIZED

◆

THE FINAL REQUEST FOR YOUR SUPPORT

While Sen. Norm Coleman was running for office, he made a promise to this columnist that, if elected, he would work to have the African American slaves recognized who helped to build the U.S. Capitol.

The Urban Youth Republican Advisory, since that promise, has met with Sen. Coleman, and he has agreed to sign on to the following legislation:

S. CON. RES. 17: Establishing a special task force to recommend an appropriate recognition for the slave laborers who worked on the construction of the United States Capitol. (Introduced in Senate)

Mr. Santorum submitted the following concurrent resolution, which was referred to the Committee on Rules and Administration:

Whereas the United States Capitol stands as a symbol of democracy, equality, and freedom to the entire world;

Whereas the year 2003 marks the 203rd anniversary of the opening of this historic structure for the first session of Congress to be held in the new Capital City;

Whereas slavery was not prohibited throughout the United States until the ratification of the 13th amendment to the Constitution in 1865;

Whereas prior to that date, African American slave labor was both legal and common in the District of Columbia and the adjoining States of Maryland and Virginia;

Whereas public records attest to the fact that African American slave labor was used in the construction of the United States Capitol;

Whereas public records further attest to the fact that the five-dollar-per-month payment for that African American slave labor was made directly to slave owners and not to the laborer; and

Whereas African Americans made significant contributions and fought bravely for freedom during the American Revolutionary War;

Now, therefore, be it Resolved by the Senate (the House of Representatives concurring), that

1. The Majority Leader of the Senate and the Speaker of the House of Representatives shall establish a special task force to include the Historian of the Senate, the Historian of the House of Representatives, the Architect of the Capitol, and the Librarian of Congress, to study the history and contributions of these slave laborers in the construction of the United States Capitol; and

2. such special task force shall produce a summary document of the contributions of slave laborers and available research for the public, and shall recommend to the Majority Leader of the Senate and the Speaker of the House of Representatives an appropriate recognition for these slave laborers which could be displayed in a prominent location in, or near, the United States Capitol.

This resolution is important. Contact your U.S. Senator and advise him/her to support this resolution. Offer your letter of support to me at mnbrc@hotmail.com

THE PRAYER FOR BLESSINGS

I will not die without being everything God wants me to be, without having everything God wants me to have. Jesus Christ made it possible that no matter what I have done, no matter who I am, God will turn my life into something I never imagined. All I have to do is believe that Christ died and lives for the forgiveness of all my mistakes. I made the choice to receive Christ into my life. And that I can repent, turn away from and walk away from my mistakes. No one can prevent me from being what God wants me to be, or have. I am willing to share with others the love, joy, peace and kindness God has given my spirit. The love of Christ has changed my life. I shall die, however; my soul shall live forever with God. I will have peace and freedom, remembering nothing in the world left behind. Having peace and waiting for Christ to take me into God's home. What a glorious day at death. My soul shall live forever with God.

At one time the Devil had me down with blessings of the world. Now, I have vision, strength, confidence and security from God. With God, I cannot be congested. I no longer go to Church on Sunday, yet conform to the world upon leaving. I shall follow my mother and all other children of God to Heaven. There is going to be a glorious reunion. We all shall be Angels with God.

Every morning God allows me to open my eyes, let me say thank you. Let me say, today, do with my life whatever you want Lord, and I shall go into that day doing the best that I can, not worried about anything, not letting the enemy take my love, joy and peace with the things in the world. For today, I live for Christ. Today, I move closer to God and eternal life. Today, I am blessed. Amen.

978-0-595-40033-1
0-595-40033-7